W9-BIQ-962

# SERIES 205

In this book, we will look at
wild woodland blooms, meteor showers
and May Day celebrations, as we
explore the beauty of the spring.

LADYBIRD BOOKS

UK | USA | Canada | Ireland | Australia
India | New Zealand | South Africa

Ladybird Books is part of the Penguin Random House group of companies
whose addresses can be found at global.penguinrandomhouse.com.

www.penguin.co.uk    www.puffin.co.uk    www.ladybird.co.uk

Penguin
Random House
UK

First published 2020
002
Copyright © Ladybird Books Ltd, 2020
Printed in Italy
A CIP catalogue record for this book is available from the British Library
ISBN: 978–0–241–41618–1
All correspondence to:
Ladybird Books
Penguin Random House Children's
One Embassy Gardens, 8 Viaduct Gardens
London SW11 7BW

MIX
Paper from
responsible sources
FSC® C018179

# What to Look For in
# Spring

## A Ladybird Book

Written by Elizabeth Jenner

Illustrated by Natasha Durley

# Lighter days are coming

"Chiff-chaff! Chiff-chaff!" Can you hear that call? The chiffchaffs are returning to the shores of the United Kingdom from southern Europe and Africa, where they have spent the winter. These birds start to arrive at the beginning of March, and their song is one of the first signs of spring. Many other birds will soon join them, including wheatears, swallows, martins, warblers, nightingales and swifts. Watch for them flying overhead now that the cold winter weather is over.

The beginning of spring is traditionally marked at the point where day and night become the same length. This happens when the sun shines directly over the equator – an imaginary line that goes round the centre of the earth between the North and South Pole. This usually occurs between 19 and 21 March and is known as the "spring equinox". From this time onwards, the days will grow longer than the nights, because the northern half of the planet will spend more time facing the sun.

The weather will also become warmer. The nights might still be cold, and you might see some frost on the ground on a chilly morning, but the temperatures will gradually rise as the natural world wakes up after the long, dark winter.

# A chorus of seabirds

Now that spring is here, the noisy seabirds have come back to the coast. Birds like these puffins and guillemots, as well as northern gannets and kittiwakes, spent the winter out at sea. Now, as the weather gets warmer, they are returning to the familiar cliffs and coastlines to live in big groups called "breeding colonies". Here, they will build nests and burrows in order to lay their eggs and hatch their babies, or "chicks", in the safety of a group.

The puffin is one of the easiest birds to spot. Sometimes known as the "clown among seabirds", it has a black head with pale cheeks and bright orange legs. During the spring, a puffin's large bill becomes brightly coloured to help it attract a mate – but it isn't just used for showing off! It is also perfectly designed for catching and carrying fish. There is a layer of tiny spines hidden inside the bill that helps the puffin to hold caught fish in place as it dives for more.

Puffins usually choose the same mate every year. The birds come ashore in pairs – one male and one female – and together they dig a burrow. The female then lays an egg inside the burrow, and the pair take it in turns to sit on the egg and keep it warm. When the egg hatches, the parents stay with the chick and feed it until it is grown up and ready to fly. Then they will leave the burrow, and the young puffin will make its way to the sea.

# Spring comes to the woodland

After the cold and dark of winter, new life can be found blooming in the woodlands. Plants are responding to the increase of sunlight and warmer temperatures, pushing up fresh green shoots and bursting into flower. From the dainty white stars of wood anemones to deep purple sweet violets and the frilly shoots of dog's mercury, the woodland floor is a place of colour and activity.

Beneath the leaves, things are just as busy. As the weather gets warmer, spotted red ladybirds wake from their winter sleep. They become more active and start to search among the new green leaves for aphids to eat. Then they mate and look for suitable places to lay their eggs.

Other species of beetle are also starting to emerge. Deathwatch beetles spend the winter as white, caterpillar-like larvae, hidden deep inside rotting wood. When spring arrives, they bore their way out of the wood and transform into adult beetles. The deathwatch beetle's name comes from the sinister tapping noise it makes against wood as it tries to attract a mate. Some people used to believe that to hear this sound in nature was a sign of approaching death.

1. Stinking hellebore
2. Sweet violet
3. Deathwatch beetle
4. Wood anemone
5. Seven-spot ladybird
6. Dog's mercury

# "As mad as a March hare"

These brown hares are putting on an energetic display. They run, scamper and chase each other all over the fields. They jump high in the air, and sometimes they stand bolt upright and use their front legs to box with each other. But what is it that makes them behave in this way?

March is the month in which most brown hares look for a mate. This is called "peak season". During this time, the male hare – called a "buck" or "jack" – tries to find a suitable female, known as a "doe" or "jill".

In order to do this, the buck must fight off competitors to convince the doe that he is the best choice of partner. He does this by showing off – running and leaping to show the doe how healthy he is. If a doe does not want to mate with him, she will attack him and box with him to send him away.

At any other time of the year, you would be lucky to see a brown hare. They are usually shy creatures, and spend the day hidden in a dip in the ground called a "form", only coming out after dark. The temporary and unusual behaviour of the brown hares during the spring season is the inspiration behind the phrase "as mad as a March hare".

# Cherry tree blossom

Some of the trees are beginning to wake up, too. If they have shed their leaves for the winter, they are known as a "deciduous" tree. The arrival of spring means that they will start to grow new buds, leaves and flowers. Some, such as the cherry tree, will produce soft pink and white blossoms.

Blossoms are important for cherry trees. The big, fragrant blooms attract insects, like bees, which drink the sweet nectar found inside the flowers. While the bee is drinking, some of the dusty pollen sticks to its body. The bee then carries the pollen to a different flower, where it comes into contact with a special part of the flower – an organ known as the "pistil". Once the pistil has received the pollen from a different plant, the flower can then develop into fruit. This process is called "pollination".

Without the help of bees and other insects, trees wouldn't be able to grow the fruit and seeds that allow them to reproduce. But the bees must work fast! Although the blossom is a striking sight, it won't last for long. Each tree will only bloom for around a week.

# Daffodils and butterflies

In early spring, look for the bright yellow brimstone butterfly flitting along hedges in search of nectar. The brimstone is one of the first butterflies to emerge each year. While other species of hibernating butterfly wait for warmer weather, the brimstone spends the winter as an adult, hiding among ivy leaves so it is ready to fly as soon as spring arrives.

Another sunny sign of spring is the wild daffodil. These distinctive flowers, with their big trumpets, can be seen almost everywhere in March. Due to the time of year that they bloom, the daffodil's cheerful appearance has come to symbolize rebirth and new beginnings.

Daffodils grow from bulbs in the ground. The bulbs spend the winter buried in the soil, storing up all the nutrients and energy that the plant will need to grow. When the temperature begins to rise, they push slim green shoots up through the earth's surface, followed eventually by a stalk with a flower bud.

It's not just daffodils and butterflies that are out and about at this time of year. As daffodils spring up in hedgerows and gardens, cyclists, runners and walkers take to the roads and paths, getting out to enjoy the spring weather, too.

# The skilful stoat

This Irish stoat stands perfectly still, waiting to spot her prey with her beady black eyes. Back in her den, a spring litter of twelve babies, or "kits", are waiting for her to bring them food. It is fortunate for them that she is a skilful hunter!

Irish stoats use their keen eyesight and excellent sense of smell to track their prey, both above the ground and under it. On land, they hunt mice, rats, birds, rabbits and insects. Once a stoat has identified its prey, it will pounce and attack with one single, strong bite to the back of the neck.

Stoats are also good climbers and swimmers. They will scale trees to reach birds' eggs and swim to catch fish in rivers. They will even eat winter nuts and berries, if some can still be found and nothing else is available.

Each Irish stoat has its own territory, in which it hunts its prey and makes a den to live in. After twelve weeks with their mother, this stoat's kits will be fully grown and ready to leave the den to find their own territories.

# April showers

It's easy to get caught in the rain in spring! Sudden heavy downpours can come along with very little warning. Often known as "April showers", they happen at this time of year because the weather pattern changes, with strong winds and rain brought in from the Atlantic Ocean. In the course of one day, there can be both warm spring sunshine and winter sleet and snow.

However, as an old saying goes, "April showers bring May flowers". Rain is good news for the plants that need lots of water to help them produce flowers later in the season. So, if April has been very wet, a beautiful blooming May is sure to follow.

It's not just the plants that love these wet conditions. Look for tiny young frogs emerging from ponds. They started life as frogspawn in the ponds of late winter, and spent the early spring as tadpoles. Now, they have grown legs and are becoming fully formed froglets, getting ready to climb out of the water and explore their new world.

# The season of new life

Springtime is a busy time on farms as it is lambing and calving season – a time when most sheep and cows give birth. In fields all across the country, fluffy lambs are leaping about and calves with wobbly legs are following their mothers, asking to be fed.

Farmers who have flocks of sheep and herds of cows must be constantly on the alert, as they may need to help with births at any time of the day or night. Most cows give birth to one calf at a time, but sheep often have twins or even triplets. Newborn animals and their mothers need a lot of care and attention from farmers to make sure they stay warm, fed and healthy.

After giving birth, the mother sheep, or "ewe", will lick and clean the lamb until it is able to stand on its own feet. Once the lamb stands up, the ewe encourages it to feed on milk from her udders. During this time, the ewe learns what her lamb smells like. Once they are both back with the flock, the ewe will use her sense of smell to recognize her offspring in the field and make sure that it is always looked after. This process between ewe and lamb is called "imprinting".

# Shooting stars

In late April, the night sky fills with shooting sparks of light. These are the April Lyrids, a meteor shower that takes place every year in the skies above the northern hemisphere.

The Lyrids meteor shower is one of the oldest known showers, and was first recorded as far back as 2,700 years ago, in ancient China. If you are lucky enough to be outside on a dark, clear night when the shower is at its height, you could see up to 20 meteors fall every hour.

The meteor shower is caused by Comet Thatcher, which journeys around the sun. A comet is a cloud of ice and dust that sheds particles of rock as it moves through space. Every year, the earth crosses the path of Comet Thatcher, and the particles from the comet hurtle into earth's upper atmosphere. As the rocks and dust enter our atmosphere, they burn up and streak brightly across the sky as meteors.

# Nest-building at the lake

Down by the lake, it is time to build nests. Look for pairs of male and female moorhens, with their bright red and yellow beaks and green legs, down by the water. They are busy finding twigs, which they will use to build their untidy nests in the reeds beside the water. Once a pair's nest is built, the female moorhen lays about eight eggs, at the rate of one per day. After about three weeks, the moorhen chicks will hatch. Both parents will stay with the nest for the entire time, and will fiercely defend it against intruders.

Meanwhile, on the water, the great crested grebes are putting on a show! The amazing black-and-orange ruffs and black ear tufts, called "tippets", are grown by the birds in preparation for a special springtime dance, which will help the grebes to impress their intended mates.

During the dance, a male and a female grebe face each other in the water, darting their heads from side to side and occasionally turning with a flick of the tail. Then, they drop low into the water and slide towards each other. Finally, they each dive to pick up a clump of weeds in their bill, and then rush towards each other. Chest to chest, they paddle furiously to stay upright in the water, while shaking the weeds in their bills. After this energetic weed-dance is over, the two grebes are officially a pair.

# Bluebells in the woods

These bright blue flowers are a brief but brilliant sight in the woods. Bluebells flower in the spring to make the most of the bright sunlight before it is blocked out by new leaves growing on the trees above. Sometimes, thousands of bluebells grow closely together in one spot, forming a beautiful blue carpet that suddenly appears, as if by magic.

Like daffodils, bluebells grow from bulbs in the soil. After the bulbs have grown shoots and burst into flower, the plants die back and produce small black seeds in pods on the flower stem. As the sunlight overhead gradually disappears, the seed pods open and the new seeds scatter. The bulbs then stay in the earth and wait for spring to return the following year.

You can often smell another springtime plant that likes to grow in the woods before you see it! Wild garlic has a fresh, pungent scent and it grows in abundance on the damp woodland floor. It, too, grows from a bulb and flowers early, spreading its crowns of white stars, to make the most of the spring light. The flat leaves of wild garlic can be picked and eaten raw, or added to soups and stews for extra flavour.

1. Wild garlic
2. Red mason bee
3. Common bluebell
4. Comma butterfly
5. Wild garlic

# Orange-tip butterflies

The orange-tip butterfly appears in early spring. The orange colour on the tips of its wings is a warning to any predators, including birds. The orange flash sends a false signal, suggesting that the butterfly is poisonous and should be avoided. Only the males have orange wingtips, so look for the females with their short, black tips too.

This female orange-tip butterfly is laying her eggs on a garlic mustard plant. She lays one egg at a time. After a few days, each egg will turn a deep orange colour, before eventually hatching into a green caterpillar.

The caterpillar will stay on the plant and feed on it throughout the summer. When the autumn comes, it will leave the plant to hide in the bushes, and then it will spend the winter inside a hard shell called a "chrysalis". Next spring, it will emerge from the chrysalis as an adult butterfly, ready to fly among the flowers and feed on their nectar.

Orange-tip butterflies feed from many spring flowers, including the "snake's head fritillary", whose petals look like snakeskin. This plant flowers in wild meadows in April, although it is not as common as it once was, because there are fewer wild meadows for it to grow in.

1. Garlic mustard
2. Male orange-tip butterfly
3. Snake's head fritillary
4. Female orange-tip butterfly
5. Orange-tip butterfly eggs

# May Day

May Day is celebrated each year on 1 May. This ancient springtime festival has roots in many cultures in the northern hemisphere, and is a time to welcome in the spring, along with the light, warmth and fertility of the season.

Throughout the centuries, May Day has been celebrated with a whole range of traditions, including festivals, dancing, singing and cake. Many towns and villages in the United Kingdom celebrate with a maypole, round which children wind colourful ribbons during a series of complicated, patterned dances. Each dance creates a new pattern of ribbons at the top of the pole. In some places, a May Queen is crowned, or Morris dancers perform with bells and sticks.

Another common sight on May Day is the delicate white-and-pink blossom on hawthorn hedges. The hawthorn is also known as the "May tree", because of the month in which it blooms. After insects have pollinated the flowers, the blooms will grow deep red fruits called "haws". The dense, thorny branches make very good hedges, and lots of birds love to nest in them.

1.  Ox-eye daisy
2.  Meadow buttercup
3.  Common hawthorn fruit, or haws
4.  Common hawthorn blossom

# Garden visitors

New leaves and lots of rain are good news for one particular type of minibeast: slugs. These slimy creatures love to eat the fresh shoots of many different vegetables and herbs – although people who have gardens are not often happy to share! Slugs can do a lot of damage to a garden in the spring, and gardeners resort to many creative measures to try to keep them out.

Slugs are molluscs that slide along the ground using one big, muscly foot. A slug uses the tentacles on its head to sense its surroundings. Since slugs are mostly made of water, they produce a protective mucus to stop themselves from drying out. This is why they prefer the wet weather. Look for their slime trails crisscrossing the paving stones after a rain shower.

Although the eating habits of slugs make these creatures unpopular with gardeners, they play an important part in the garden ecosystem, by eating away lots of rotting material and fungi.

1. Kerry spotted slug
2. European black slug
3. Lemon slug
4. Netted slug
5. European red slug
6. Worm slug
7. Common garden slug
8. Yellow slug
9. Dusky slug

# Down by the river

As the weather gets warmer, so do the natural springs of water across the country. This wild swimmer has come down to the river for her first dip of the year. She has a few companions, including a mallard and her ducklings.

Earlier in the spring, the mother duck built her nest safely away from the river, then laid her eggs. When her ducklings first hatched, she waited a few hours for them to learn to stand and walk. Then, early the next morning, she led them all down to the water. She will now stay with them for roughly two months, keeping them warm and teaching them how to feed on pondweed and insects, until they are strong enough to live on their own.

The bright flashes of colour above the water are demoiselle damselflies and dragonflies. They are swooping low over the water to catch tiny midges and mosquitoes. Dragonflies are the stunt pilots of the insect world. With their four strong wings, they can fly backwards as well as forwards, and they are one of the fastest insects in the United Kingdom, with a top flight-speed of 30 miles per hour (48 km/h).

# Songbirds at dawn

It is early on a May morning. First light is starting to creep over the horizon. Over the stillness comes the call of a bird. Then comes another, and then another. Soon it seems as though every bird in the trees – from the blackbird and the robin to the wren and the chaffinch – is singing and chattering in conversation.

This is the dawn chorus. Birds prefer to sing at this time because the air is usually still, so the sound carries further. For the most part, only male songbirds sing. They call out to attract mates, and to warn other birds away from their territory. The dawn chorus happens all through the spring, but is at its loudest in May, when the birds' breeding season is at its peak.

Among the trees that these birds like to perch in is the ash. One of the last trees to flower in spring, the ash can live for up to 400 years. Many birds, bats and insects like to live in the shelter of its wood and on its branches.

1.  Common chaffinch
2.  European wren
3.  European tree sparrow
4.  Common blackbird
5.  European robin

# The garden at night

As night falls over the back gardens of city houses, some fox cubs come out to play. They are exploring, watched carefully by their mother.

Foxes give birth in the spring, but their cubs do not leave the warm home, or "den", until they are at least four weeks old. This is because they are born blind and deaf, so need to stay cuddled close to their mother and feed on her milk. These cubs are now six weeks old, and can start to venture away from the safety of the den and learn to hunt and scavenge.

Foxes adapt very well to their environment, and will eat whatever is on offer. They are just as happy to live in a city as in woodland. They will eat voles, birds, rabbits, insects, beetles, fruit, vegetables and even takeaway leftovers. They are nocturnal, so watch out for their rusty white-tipped tails slipping through your garden after dark.

Another night-time visitor is a little pricklier. The hedgehog is a solitary creature with up to 7,000 spines on its back, which it can raise for protection if it feels at risk of attack. This hedgehog has come out to look for beetles, earthworms and caterpillars to eat. It may have little legs, but it can walk up to 2 miles (3 km) every night in search of food.

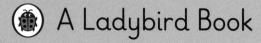

# A Ladybird Book

collectable books for curious kids

## What to Look For in
## Spring
A Ladybird Book

What to Look For in Spring

9780241416181

## What to Look For in
## Summer
A Ladybird Book

What to Look For in Summer

9780241416204